FINANCIAL LITERACY: YOUR GATEWAY TO BECOMING ELITE

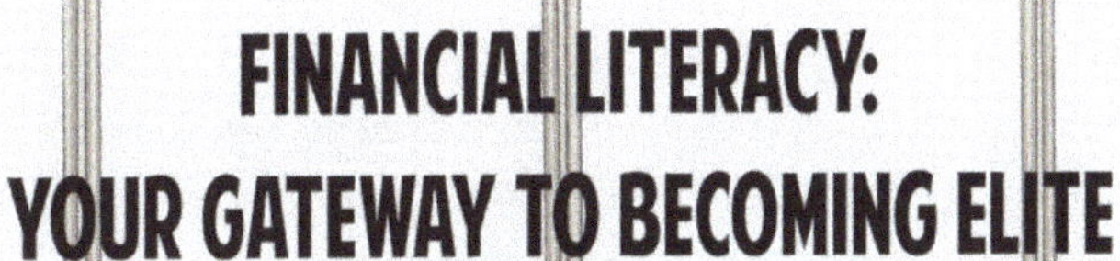

Written by Miguel Hartford

Illustrated by Sara Abbas

Lovett Press International
214-350-1696

ISBN: 9798327944961

To see other books by this author, visit:
Hartfordbooks.com

Contact the author directed by:
Migueldenisia@gmail.com

Illustrator: Sara Abbas
saraabbasart@gmail.com

Dedication

To everyone who experiences
better financial success after reading this.

Table of Contents

What is Financial Literacy, and Why is it Important?

Financial Literacy is the ability to understand and effectively use various financial skill including personal financial management, budgeting, and investing. It is important that people know and understand financial literacy, because this gives you the knowledge and tools to understand money in every aspect from areas like income and saving, to investing and retiring.

Saving Money

"Why should we save money?"

Saving is putting money aside for the future. It is necessary that we save money. Things happen in life that we aren't prepared for and many of things require immediate attention. This can be payment for medical issues, vehicle breakdowns, home repairs, travel for family emergencies, etc. It is important to have money set aside for unexpected problems later.

We save money to have it later. It can be for something fun, retirement, or just the unexpected. Vehicles will require money at some point. It can be a mechanical problem, a flat tire, a wreck, etc. It's smart to keep money set aside for these occurrences.

Vacations cost money. It's best to save in advance, to have a better trip. It's important to keep money saved, as life is unpredictable, and it's necessary to always have access to money.

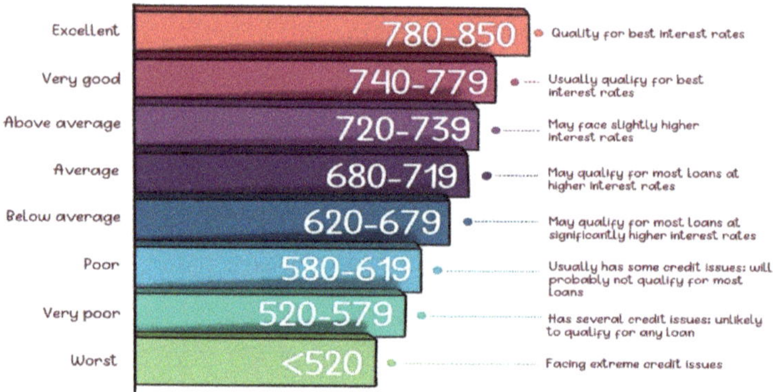

"What is a credit score and what does it mean?"

A credit score is a 3-digit number usually falling between the range of 300-850 that determines the likelihood that a person will pay their bills on time and incorporates another risk factors. The higher a person's credit score is, the better their options will be with things like loans and credit cards. This is being approved for a loan, as well as the interest rate they receive. A higher credit scores has a lower interest rate, which means the person pays back less money overall. A lower credit score has a higher interest rate, which results in paying back more money.

A Fico Score is a specific type of credit score. It is a three-digit number that is used by most of the top lenders. It is determined by the Fair Isaac Corporation.

There are different scales for credit scores. A general scale is as follows:

300- 579- Poor
580-669-Fair
670-739- Good
740799- Very Good
800-850- Excellent

There are multiple factors that affect your credit score.

- Payment history considers if someone late payments, such as paying their credit card bills or loans, on time, bankruptcies, and debt collection.
- The amount of credit used vs the amount of credit available is a factor. It is best to use only 30% of one's available credit. For example, if a person has a $1,000 credit limit, then they should not use over $300 of their credit.

- There are two types of credit, which are revolving and installment credit. Revolving credit consists of credit cards that change amounts as you spend. Installment credit is a fixed amount, such as a fixed loan for a home or vehicle that gets paid monthly and eventually ends as you pay it off. It is best to have a mixture of both.
- Another factor is the number of credit inquiries or requests a person has made. When someone requests a line of credit, this is considered a hard inquiry. It is important to not make multiple hard inquiries in a short period of time.

Credit Card

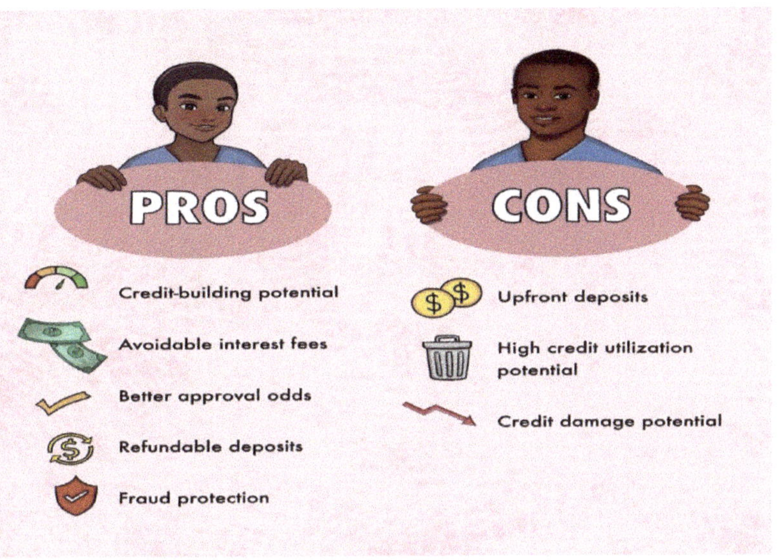

Credit cards are physical cards that can be used in person or online for purchases and payments. Traditional credit cards have a limit, and a person can use the credit card to spend up to that amount. If the credit card is paid off in full before the due date, then no interest is owed. Interest is money owed for borrowing money. Interest on a credit card is called Annual Percentage Rate or APR. Higher credit scores give a lower APR. If the credit card is not paid off before the due date, then the amount owed is added to the interest rate.

There are pros and cons to having a credit card.

Pros of credit cards:

- Building credit history
- Increase purchasing power
- Better option for hotel rooms and rental cars
- Credit card is not linked to checking or savings accounts
- Rewards such as points for hotel rooms, other perks, airline miles or cash back\
- Fraud protection

Cons of credit cards;
- Debt
- Overuse of funds

Bills and Budgeting

"All the money we would have if we didn't have to pay bills."

Every month bills are due. It is a main priority to pay required bills before spending money on anything else. This is called budgeting. You take the money you have coming in, subtract the bills and other monthly expenses that are outgoing. It is important to keep track of all bills. That is where budgeting comes in. It's necessary to know the amounts and dates of bills.

Some bills are fixed, meaning the amount is the same every month, such as most internet or cell phone bills. Water and electricity bills will vary monthly. Some months require extra money, such as colder winter months or hotter summer months, where more power is used for central air and heat, and many children and adults being home and indoors more during those seasons. In these cases, it is important to set aside extra money for these bills.

There is a 50/30/20 Rule for budgeting. This means you spend 50% of after-tax income on needs, 30% on wants and 20% on savings and debt reduction.

"Do you want it, or do you need it?"

Knowing the difference between needs versus wants seems simple, but that isn't always the case. You may need a coat, but you may not need an expensive designer coat. It's important that your wants and needs remain in your budget. Needs are the things you need to function in daily life. Rent or mortgage, utility bills, healthcare and therapy, medication, food, work uniforms or attire, and transportation or commuting. Some people confuse lifestyle with living, which results in them confusing needs and wants.

Food is a need. You may need to buy groceries, but this is buying what is affordable and in your budget. You do not need to buy steak and lobster. Fruits and vegetables are needs. Junk food and soda are not. Clothes are needs. Work uniforms or appropriate work attire is a need. Excessive name brand clothes are not a need.

Rent or a mortgage is a need, but one does not need to spend beyond their means to live in a particular place. Some people may need to downsize their apartment. Saving money on where you live can be done by having a roommate or living with family if possible.

Transportation and commuting are expensive. You should consider all options when needed. Public transportation, carpooling and even walking and riding a bike may work instead of driving sometimes. Having a vehicle that is affordable is very necessary. The monthly car note payments for a mid-level sedan, is much lower than those on a luxury SUV.

Wants are categorized as entertainment, dining out, home purchases, travel, electronics, monthly subscriptions or memberships, TV or streaming accounts, and new clothing.

When determining wants versus needs, it is important to remember the 50/30/20 Rule. Needs are 50% of income, wants are 30% and savings and debt reduction are 20%. Saving money is a need, as saving money goes towards different areas. Your savings can be used towards future emergencies, debt reduction, retirement, and other areas.

Opportunity Cost

"Sometimes you can't have both."

Opportunity cost is the loss of potential gain from other alternatives when one alternative is chosen. This means giving up one thing, to have another. We experience this all time. An example of opportunity cost is spending money on games for a PlayStation, instead of spending money on shoes, clothes, or a trip.

Being Content and Not Overspending

It is important to be happy with your life and not spend unnecessary money for no reason. This can relate to mental, emotional, and psychological issues that people experience, which can cause them to spend money to fill a void. Some people spend money because they are not happy. Them spending money is therapeutic. This leads to spending problems down the line. It is also important to not spend money to impress others. Only spend money on your needs and what you can afford (not buy) that makes you happy.

Impulse Buys and Money Habits

"Just because you can buy something, doesn't mean you can afford it."

Buying things on a whim can hurt you in the long run, so it's important to be careful. It may be a good time to buy something, and you may have the money to spare, but it's important to not be wasteful and buy things just because. It is also necessary to consider the cost of up-keep. For example, you may be able to buy a certain vehicle, but it is important to budget to the extreme. It is necessary to know about upkeep, repairs, insurance, and other costs. Plus, you must plan for the unexpected that can affect your current budgeting plans. It is important to live within your means.

A habit is a regular practice. People with good money habits make better decisions with their money, and have more money for things they really want, as well as more money in the long run. It's important to have good money habits early. This sometimes requires strong will for some people, but it will pay off.

Taxes

"How rich would we be if we didn't have to pay taxes?"

Taxes must be paid no matter what. Taxes are mandatory payments or charges paid by individuals and businesses to local, state, and national governments. There are many taxes that we pay, and taxes affect everyone differently. This includes, income tax, payroll tax, property tax, sales tax, corporate tax, estate tax and tariff. It is important to pay the correct amount of taxes owed, to avoid consequences. If property taxes aren't paid, then the property and homes can be seized, or taken by the government. If income taxes aren't paid, then one's checks can be garnished, meaning that a percentage will be taken out and paid towards those taxes.

There are different types of categories of taxes which are regressive, proportional, and progressive. Individual income tax taken out of a person's individual wages, salaries, and other income. Business income tax is taxes paid from corporations, partnerships, self-employed contractors, and small businesses. Most states have a state tax that is also paid by residents.

Regressive taxes affect people with higher incomes differently than those with lower incomes. Sales tax, payroll taxes, excise taxes and property taxes are regressive taxes. This means there is a flat rate that is paid, and this affects those who make less money more than those who make more money. Sales tax is tax that is charged for buying items at the time of a sale, such as items bought in a store. Payroll tax is a tax paid on salary and wages. Excise taxes are fixed taxes charged for specific goods and included in the price of service, such as fuel, airfare, alcohol, and tobacco. Property tax is a charge that is paid to the state for property owned, such as a house or building.

Proportional taxes are flat taxes that is applied to everyone at the same rate. This means a person is not penalized when they make more money or enter a higher tax bracket. Sales tax can also be categorized as a proportional tax, as everyone pays the same amount.

Progressive taxes change according to an individual's income, which results in an increase on those with higher incomes and earnings. Income tax is an example of a progressive tax.

Banks, Credit unions and Other Financial Institutions

"Who is keeping your money?"

Money is kept in financial institutions. Types of financial institutions are central banks, retail and commercial banks, credit unions, investment banks, brokerage firms, savings and loan associations, insurance companies, and mortgage companies.

Central banks manage and monitor all other banks. Retails banks service individuals, while commercial banks service businesses. Unlike retail banks, credit unions are nonprofit. They are owned by their members and offer the traditional services that retail banks offer. Savings and loan associations are owned by their customers or community. They offer the services that traditional banks and credit unions offer, such as checking accounts and personal loans, but their focus is on residential or home mortgages.

Investment banks assist with services on a larger scale, such as a company preparing for an IPO (Initial Public Offering), or when companies are merging. Brokerage firms assist with customers trading stocks, bonds, mutual funds, exchange-traded funds, and additional investments. Insurance companies are financial institutions that provide protection. This can be against death, disability, accidents, property damage and other occurrences that require financial protection. Mortgage companies initially provide the capital, or money to buy a house, but other mortgage companies assist in the commercial or business real estate instead.

Mortgages and Loans

Most people pay mortgages when they buy a home. This is an agreement between you and a lender, where the lender can take your property if you do not pay the money borrowed, plus the interest. Most people get a 30- year mortgage, but 10 and 15-year mortgages are also options. There are five types of home loans: conventional, jumbo, government-backed, fixed-rate and adjustable rate. A conventional loan is the most common type of home loan and has two categories: conforming and non-conforming. Conforming loans adhere to Federal Housing Finance Agency (FHA) standards, such as credit, debt, and loan size. These are covered by Fannie Mae and Freddie Mac, which are lending companies.

Non-conforming loans don't meet the standards that conforming loans do. An example is a jumbo loan, which is used to finance property that is over the amount of a conventional conforming loan. This is a high-risk loan, as it cannot be guaranteed by Fannie Mae and Freddie Mac, so the lender can lose money if the borrower does not pay the money back. Jumbo loans may have a fixed-interest rate or an adjustable rate. Fixed- interest rates have the same interest rate throughout the life of the loan. Adjustable-rate loans begin with the same interest rate for a period, and then the rate is adjusted per a benchmark index until the loan ends.

Government-backed loans are insured by an agency of the federal government. This included FHA, VA, and USDA loans. FHA loans are insured by the Federal Housing Administration. The required criteria to receive this type of loan is a minimum credit score of 58-0 with a 3.5% down payment or a minimum score of 500 with 10% down. Mortgage insurance premiums are required, which increases the cost. The amount that can be borrowed for FHA loans is much lower than that for a conventional conforming loan.

VA loans are guaranteed by the U.S. Department of Veterans Affairs. This applies to eligible members of the U.S. military and their surviving spouses. No minimum down payment, mortgage insurance or credit score apply. There is a required funding fee between 1.25-3.3% at closing.

USDA loans are guaranteed by the U.S. Department of Agriculture. These loans are designed to assist moderate to low-income borrowers buy homes in areas that are USDA-eligible. No credit score or down payment is required, but borrowers to have to pay guarantee fees.

Fixed rate mortgages have the same interest rate of the entire life of the loan. These are usually 15- or 30-year loans. Advantages of this type of loan are having a fixed monthly mortgage payment and being able to budget the mortgage expense. Disadvantages of this type of loan are higher interest rates than those on adjustable-rate loans and having to refinance or go through a change to change the interest rates and terms, to lower the interest rate.

Adjustable-rate mortgage has interest rates that change over time. It begins with a lower rate at the start of the loan for set period. Then, the rate increases or decreases. Advantages are lower introductory rates and possibly paying less over time. Disadvantages are risk of higher payment and difficulty of budgeting the mortgage payment.

Balancing Bank Accounts

It used to be simple to balance a checkbook before everything went digital. Writing a check was more time consuming and complicated than swiping a debit or credit card in a store or online. This makes it even more important to budget and know how much is in your account and how much will be taken out, so you don't end up overdrawn. Being overdrawn means you do not have enough money to cover the money being debited or taken out of your account. An overdrawn account results in overdraft fees, which are extra fees you must pay for not having enough money for the payments that were being debited out.

Debt

Debt can vary. No one likes to have debt, because it means you owe someone, and your money is obligated elsewhere until that is paid off. There is good debt and bad debt. Good debt means the debt acquired can increase your net worth or has future value. Examples of good debt are student loans, mortgages, and small business loans. All these work towards bettering your future and have value. Examples of bad debit are payday loans, automobile loans and credit card debt.

Debt to income ratio is your monthly debt payments, divides by your gross monthly income. This determines how much money lenders will lend you, and the interest rate, or percentage they will charge you. The front-end ratio includes the percentage of your income that would go to the mortgage payment, property taxes, home-owners insurance, and other home expenses. The back-end ratio consists of all other monthly debt payments such as credit cards, vehicle loans, child support, student loans, and the regularly occurring expenses, excluding utilities.

Salary

Salary is the amount of money a person receives from employment. Salary controls a person's lifestyle. It sets the tone for what a person can afford, where they live, the type of car they drive, the level of healthcare they receive, the type of food they buy, the luxuries they have and more. It's best to know the type of lifestyle you want to live and get a job with the salary that matches it. This also affects retirement, as the amount of money a person saves for retirement, comes from their salary. The more you make, the more you can save for retirement.

Having an allowance is a good way to teach young people about salary, spending and saving money. It teaches young people responsibility. It can teach saving, and good spending habits.

Self-Employment

It is great to be self-employed or an entrepreneur, which means you own your own business and get to do what you want or love to do. The pros of being self-employed means setting your own hours and schedule. Traveling when and where you want. However, it is important to know that working for yourself consists of other factors. There is no consistency with being self-employed. You may do great one week or one month, and then you may make a lot less money the following week or month.

There may be no one else to assist with bills that a sole-proprietor, or a single person who owns their business pays. There are also out of pocket costs that are more expensive, because you are paying individually not through a large group, such as health insurance and benefits.

Some people who own their own business work full time jobs to keep a consistent salary, and have benefits for now, such as health insurance, retirement, and other benefits. Others still put money into social security on their own, to receive social security and Medicare benefits when they are old enough. Full time self-employed people can also set up a 401K account, but unlike with large corporations, all the money is being put in by the person themselves, and there is no employer to match a percentage of the money being put in. This means they must put more money in.

It is also important to save and prepare for the future when you're self-employed. This requires self-discipline, as people are solely self-employed are solely depending on themselves to set their retirement goals. This means saving money for retirement and not touching it. Self-employed people can set up their own 401K or retirement account as well as deposit money into social security, but 34% of employers do not set up a retirement plan.

Commission and Bonuses

Some jobs like sales and jobs in the financial sector such as stockbrokers, pay commissions. This means the person is being paid a specific amount or percentage for a particular amount of something that is sold. If you get paid $2 for something that costs $10, and you sell 20 units, then the commission is $40. Jobs that pay commission vary, and the person is usually never paid the same amount every pay period. That means, they cannot depend on or account for money at every pay period, until their commission is set to be paid.

Bonuses are also important. Many companies give annual bonuses when they are making profits and successful or not losing money that year. Some companies give bonuses multiple times within the year, such as monthly goals reached. This can be a major help with income, or some people spend it as a reward for something they usually do not have the money for.

Giving Money to Others

Many people donate money to religions organization such as churches and religious charities, make financial donations, and give money through other forms of philanthropy. This can be done through regular budgeting such as weekly or monthly giving, or it can be seasonal or annual. It's always good to help others when you can. Sometimes it is a tax write off, meaning when you file your taxes, you get a credit for your donation.

Investing

Investing is important to make more money now, and/or for the future. It could be in stocks, bonds, mutual funds, property etc. Or it can be very long term like a 401K account, CD account, where you put money into the account, and the longer it is in there, the more of a return on investment you receive or the more money you make.

Stocks are a common form of investment. Buying stocks, is a buying an ownership stake in a publicly traded company. Like many other forms of investing, stocks are a risk. If the stock price increases, you can sell the stocks for a profit. If the stock price decreases, you can lose money.

Bonds are ways of loaning money to an entity. The investor then collects interest on the bonds. There are corporate bonds issued by companies, municipal bonds issued by the government, and the U.S. Treasury issues treasury bonds. Stocks pay a higher rate of return than bonds. The risk with bonds is the company can close or the government can default or refuse to repay its debt obligations.

Mutual funds allow you to pool money with other investors to mutually buy stocks, bonds, and other investments. This can be done passively managed, or actively managed. An actively managed fund is managed by a portfolio manager.

A certificate of deposit or CD is a low-risk investment where you give the bank a certain amount of money, for a specific amount of time and earn interest on it. If you don't withdraw the money during the term agreed with the bank, then there is no penalty, only the reward of the interest earned.

Annuities are a way of earning income during retirement. It is a form of investing in yourself as you pay money up front, for future income later. With an annuity, there is a contract between you and an insurance company. This is where a company pays you for the premiums you have paid. It is not a form of life insurance. Life insurance is paid if you die. The annuity pays your income while you are still alive.

Commodities are raw materials that can be invested in or sold. There are four categories of commodities: metals, agricultural, livestock, and energy. Metals are gold and silver and industrial metals like copper. Agricultural products are coffee, wheat, corn, and soybeans. Livestock products are cattle, sheep, livestock, poultry, and goats. Energy commodities are crude oil, petroleum products and natural gas.

There are additional forms of investments. Derivatives are financial instruments that drive their value from another asset. ETFs are Exchange-Traded Funds are like mutual funds, as they are a collection of investments that track a market index. Cryptocurrency is a type of EFT investment. Options are a more complex way to buy a stock. Hybrid Investments use the elements of equities and fixed-income securities.

Investment property can be rental houses or apartments, or leasing buildings to business owners. The person who owns the home or building receives money for rent monthly, which is a form of monthly income for the property owner.

College and Student Loans

College can be expensive. Getting a college education is great, but it important to not get too much debt or none as a result. It is good to know options. College scholarships and financial aid are important. Some tuition and fees are lower at other schools. There are also other options such as online classes with lower fees and starting at community colleges with much lower tuition costs. It is important to do your research.

Student loans should be a last resort. Student loans have a daily interest rate, which means every day, the interest is calculated by the amount owed. Credit cards charge a monthly interest rate. This is why it takes people so many years to pay back student loans. A school being popular, does not mean it is a good choice. In the real world, people will come from many colleges all over the country, and most college graduates will all make a salary within the same range. The best college choice is a school that won't result in you having any debt, or not much.

Another option is parents of a college student getting a personal loan when their child starts college. This may be a good option for some people, as they get the money up front for what the student's tuition and expenses will be at the beginning of their 4-year career. This allows a set amount borrowed, and it can be paid off within the number of years set such as 5-7 years.

Retirement Plans-401K, Pension, and other Accounts

Although the future is far away for many, it is important that we plan for it in advance. Millions of people do not properly plan financially for the future, and when the time to retire comes, they do not have enough money to retire happily. It is important to know where your money will come from for retirement, how much you currently have, how much you will need, and exactly what you need to do to achieve your desired retirement goal amount in time.

Some jobs have a different form of retirement called a pension. At one time, this was the most common form of retirement plan. A pension is an employee retirement plan that allows an employee to deposit money over time for retirement. When an employee has been with a company over a certain time, the pension will grow. When the employee reaches the required age of retirement, they will receive a monthly check until their death. The pension retirement plan is given with careers like teachers, firefighters, state workers, university workers and other companies that may still offer this form of retirement.

Most jobs offer a 401K, which is a retirement account that takes a portion of each paycheck and puts it into an account. In most cases, the employer matches the amount the employee puts in, to a certain percentage. This is one of the best types of security for retirement. The 401K is pre-tax, and Roth 401K is after tax. A 403B account is similar. With these accounts, you can withdraw money under certain circumstances, such as home repairs related to weather damages, home foreclosure, higher education expenses, and medical reasons. If an early withdrawal is made, it is with a penalty, meaning you pay a percentage for taking money out before your retirement age. Unlike pensions, the 401K is a set amount, and it is up to the person's discretion, as to how much money to take out.

This requires money management skills, as a 401K can run out quickly, and some people are not sure how much money to take out.

Annuities is another form of retirement payments. This is where the previous lump sum payment or series of payments made, result in you receiving payments for retirement. Indexed Universal Life Insurance or IUL is a type of permanent life insurance that offers a cash value component along with a death benefit. This type of retirement plan is great as it covers multiple areas.

The Fab Four of Retirement

There is a check list of ways to retire effectively. It is important to plan, because if you fail to plan, then you plan to fail. I call this check list the Fab Four of Retirement, as it falls into four categories: Retirement Income, Healthcare, Safe Investing, and Estate Planning. If these four areas are invested into, your retirement will be smooth and successful.

Retirement income consists of social security and annuities. Social security gives a base retirement income monthly for those who put money into the social system. Annuities can also offset or provide a gap of monthly payments for income.

Healthcare is mandatory for retirees to have. Medicare is government funded healthcare that is provided, and it covers the large part of healthcare for retirees. This helps to not pay out of pocket, which leaves additional money for other things. Long-Term Care Insurance is important to have as you get older. This is to cover long term medical care that may be required, and will avoid you depleting, or spending your savings.

Safe investing consists of Fixed Indexed Annuities. This is where your investment is linked to a stock market index, while also protecting your principal, or original amount that was invested. The goal of this is to increase your retirement savings, while eliminating the market risk of you losing your investment.

Estate Planning involves life insurance and final expense insurance. Life insurance is money that is paid overtime, to make sure your beneficiaries or loved ones, can receive money after your death. This is to ensure that they are safe with a stable income. It is also a way for them to build money of their own. Final Expense Insurance is to cover funeral costs and eliminate stress, so that your family does not have to pay for the funeral costs out of pocket.

An IUL, or Indexed Universal Life Insurance, can cover multiple avenues, including life insurance, long term care, and annuities. You can put as much money as you would like into it monthly, but the more you put into it, the more you will receive from it. For example, if a person puts $500 a month into an IUL, they will have over a million dollars in it in 30 years. That's a great investment.

Racial Disparity and Retirement

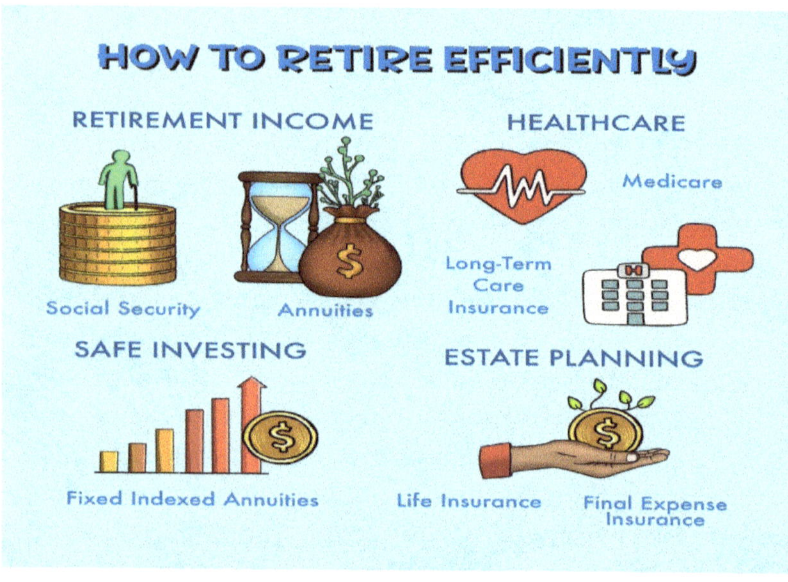

There is a racial disparity when it comes to the preparation for retirement. 83% of African Americans lack retirement assets for long-term. The median net worth for Caucasian Americans is $331,700 which is close to 10 times higher than that of African-Americans, which is- $36,200. Also, 46% of African Americans depend on soc

ial security for 90% or more of income vs Whites who depend on 35%. There is also a disparity among Latino Americans as only 34% believe they have saved enough for retirement. Only 30% of Latino population is participating in a retirement program. It is important that these numbers are changed for the better.

Drafting a Future Budget

When the time to retire comes, it is important to know how much money you will need a month and what your life expectancy is. Social security benefits and a pension will come every month for the rest of your life. However, that is not the case for a 401K, 403B and other accounts with a full amount. People who have these accounts often are not sure how much to take out of these accounts monthly, as they do not want to run out of money. The life expectancy today is longer than it previously was. So, it is important to maximize your life expectancy and calculate how much money you will need every month for the rest of your life and ensure that the needed amount will be available.

It is important to have enough money when you retire, so you need to know how much things will cost and what you will need to pay for when you retire. It is important to complete a check list of important questions. Do you own a home or property? Will your mortgage be paid off by the time you retire? How much will your expenses cost? Have you considered a cost-of-living increase? Will you be able to afford home repairs and maintenance? Are you prepared for emergencies? Will you still owe payments on your vehicle? Will you be able to afford another vehicle.

Real World Examples

Kids who are too young to have jobs can experience financial literacy in different situations. For example, money can be given for chores, which correlates to income, and good grades, which correlates to bonuses. This teaches earning money. The money can be deposited into an account or mobile payment service. This shows them how money works personally, and teaches different avenues such as saving, spending, and investing if they would like.

It is important that young adults and people building careers map out their futures. You must know the salary you will receive and the expenses you need to cover. There are different costs of living in different cities. You should know what the income needed to live comfortably is in your city. It is also important to be prepared to pay bills on one income if needed.

Resources

11 Common Types of Investments and How They Work. (2023,

June 23).

Smartassest. https://smartasset.com/investing
/types-of-investment

CenturionWealth, & Ashford, K. (2022, September
20). *Forbes: 34% of entrepreneurs have no
retirement savings plan.* Centurion Wealth - Top
Wealth
Advisor. https://centurionwealth.com/forbes-
34-of-entrepreneurs-have-no-retirement-
savings-plan/

Equifax. (2023). *What is a credit
score?* https://www.equifax.com/personal/ed

ucation/credit/score/articles/-/learn/what-is-a-credit-score/

Discover. (2023, September 13). *What are the advantages of a credit card?* Discover. https://www.discover.com/credit-cards/card-smarts/what-are-the-advantages-of-credit-cards/

Tax Foundation. (2024, February 23). *Regressive Tax | TaxEDU Glossary.* https://taxfoundation.org/taxedu/glossary/regressive-tax/

Crpc, S. P. (2024, May 23). *Unlocking your retirement potential: A guide to Managing Retirement Taxes | The Annuity Expert.* The Annuity Expert. https://www.annuityexpertadvice.co

m/calculator/retirement-taxes-and-penalties-
calculator/

Dehan, A. (2024, February 9). *5 types of mortgage loans
for homebuyers.*
Bankrate. https://www.bankrate.com/mortga
ges/types-of-mortgages/

Fay, B. *Good Debt vs. Bad Debt - Types of Good and Bad
Debts.* (2024, January 5).
Debt.org. https://www.debt.org/advice/good
-vs-bad/

Fernando, J. (2024, April 12). *Financial literacy: What it
is, and why it is so important to teach teens.*
Investopedia. https://www.investopedia.com
/terms/f/financial-literacy.asp

Gorton, D. (2024, May 23). *Taxes Definition: types, who pays, and why.*

Investopedia. https://www.investopedia.com /terms/t/taxes.asp

Guzman, E., & Vulimiri, M. (2015). Making policy work for people.

In *www.globalpolicysolutions.org*. https://www. globalpolicysolutions.org

Horton, M. (2023, September 20). *Different types of financial institutions.*

Investopedia. https://www.investopedia.com /ask/answers/061615/what-are-major- categories-financial-institutions-and-what-are- their-primary-roles.asp

Kenton, W. (2022, July 17). *Strategic Financial Management: definition, benefits, and example.* Investopedia. https://www.investopedia.com /terms/s/strategic-financial-management.asp

Kurt, D. (2024, April 19). *Retirement annuities: Know the pros and cons.* Investopedia. https://www.investopedia.com /articles/retirement/121416/retirement- annuities-know-pros-and-cons.asp

Lin, N. (2023, October 10). *Half of Hispanic adults not prepared for retirement, LIMRA reports | PLANADVISER.* PLANADVISER. https://www.planadviser.co m/half-hispanic-adults-not-prepared- retirement-limra-reports/#:~:text=LIMRA%20found%20that%2

034%25%20of,lower%20than%20the%20nation

al%20average

Luthi, B. (2020, October 11). *What is a Government-
Backed
Mortgage?* Experian. https://www.experian.co
m/blogs/ask-experian/what-is-a-government-
backed-mortgage/

Markowitz, A. (2024, February 5). *The Racial
Retirement Gap in 7 Facts.*
AARP. https://www.aarp.org/retirement/pla
nning-for-retirement/info-2023/racial-savings-
wealth-gap.html

Pant, P. (2022b, June 20). What is the difference
between wants and needs? *The*

Balance. https://www.thebalancemoney.com/how-to-separate-wants-and-needs-453592

Powers, S. (2023, December 15). *What is Indexed Universal Life Insurance (IUL)?* Investopedia. https://www.investopedia.com/articles/insurance/09/indexed-universal-life-insurance.asp#:~:text=Indexed%20universal%20life%20(IUL)%20insurance%20is%20a%20form%20of%20permanent,to%20a%20fixed%2Drate%20account.

Wells, L. (2024, February 20). *What is a debt-to-income ratio for a mortgage?* Bankrate. https://www.bankrate.co

m/mortgages/why-debt-to-income-matters-in-

mortgages/#what-is

Whiteside, E. (2024, February 26). *The 50/30/20 budget

rule explained with examples.*

Investopedia. https://www.investopedia.com

/ask/answers/022916/what-502030-budget-

rule.asp

Wood, K., & Buczynski, B. (2023, December 21). *Jumbo

Loans: When a Regular Mortgage Isn't Enough.*

Nerd

Wallet. https://www.nerdwallet.com/article/

mortgages/jumbo-loans-what-you-need-to-

know